THIS JOURNAL BELONGS TO

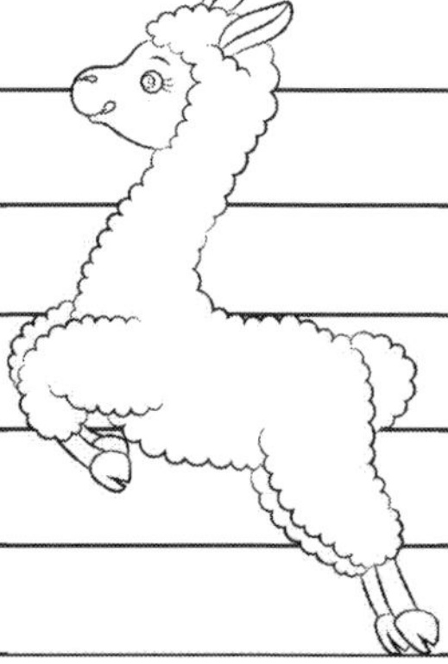

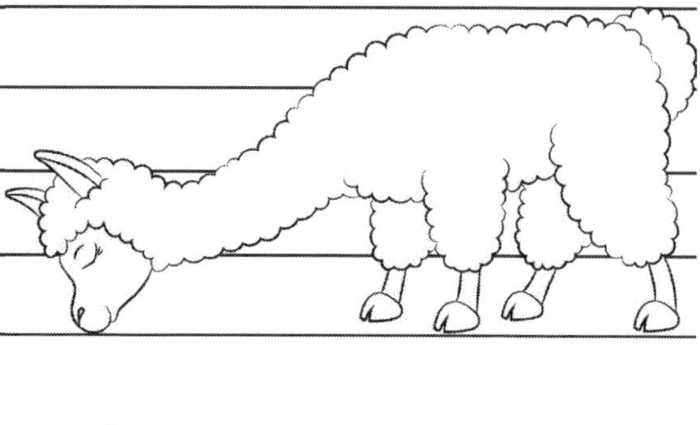

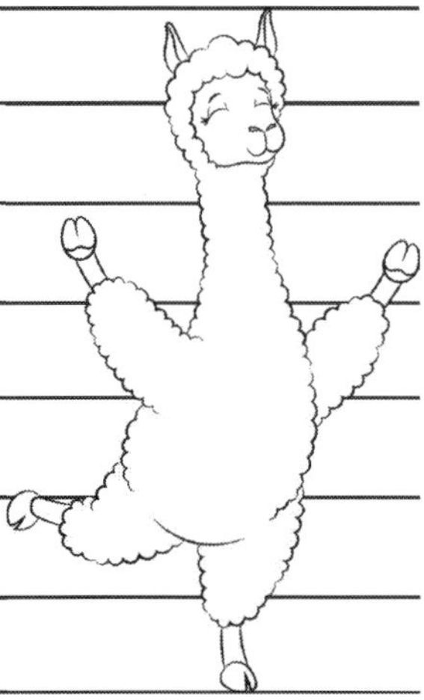

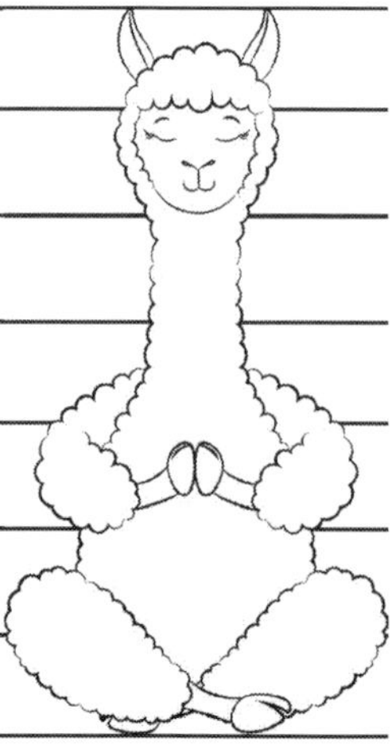

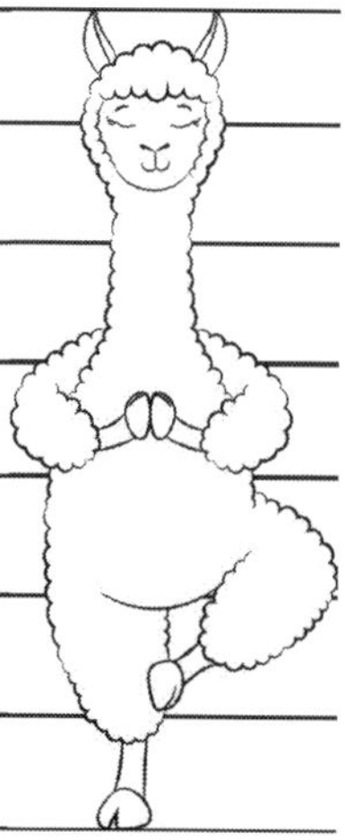

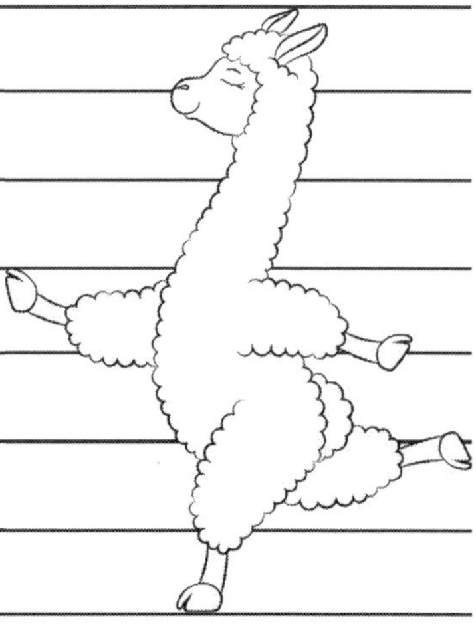

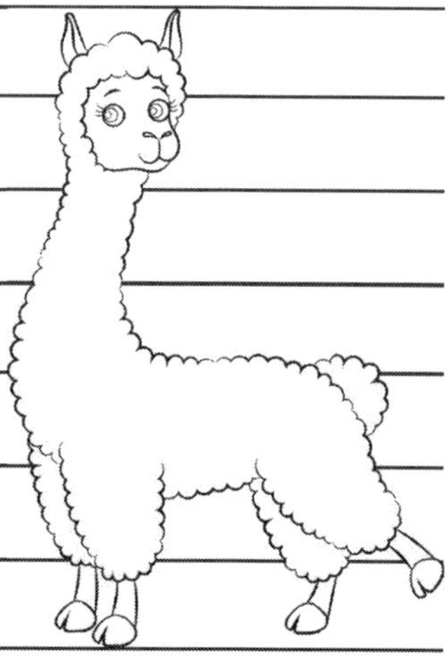

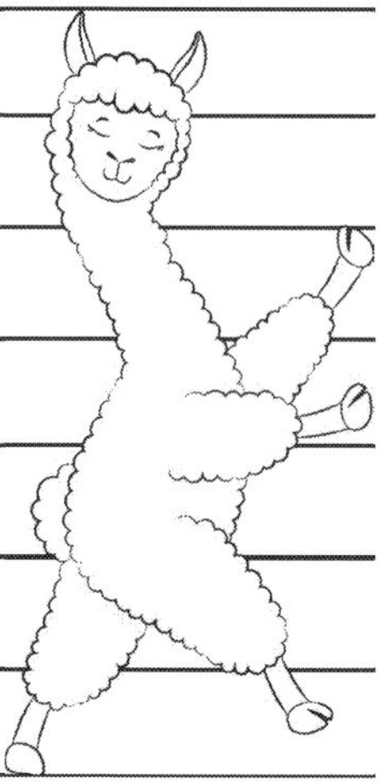

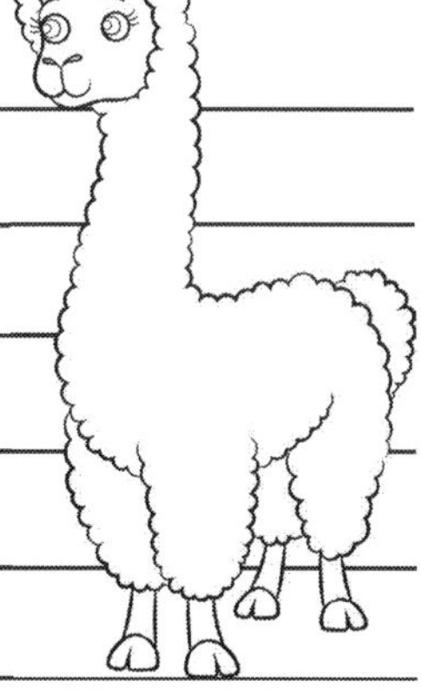

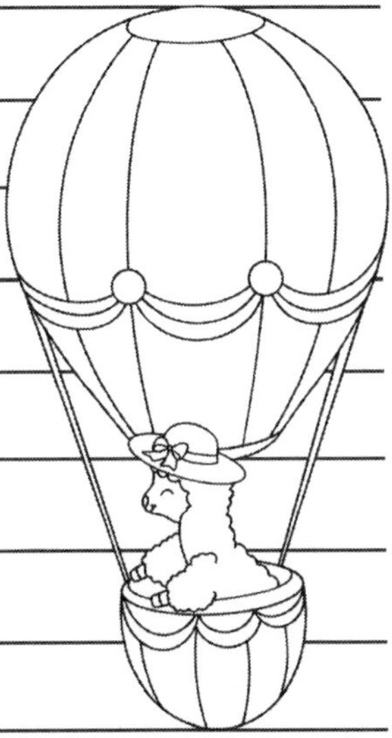

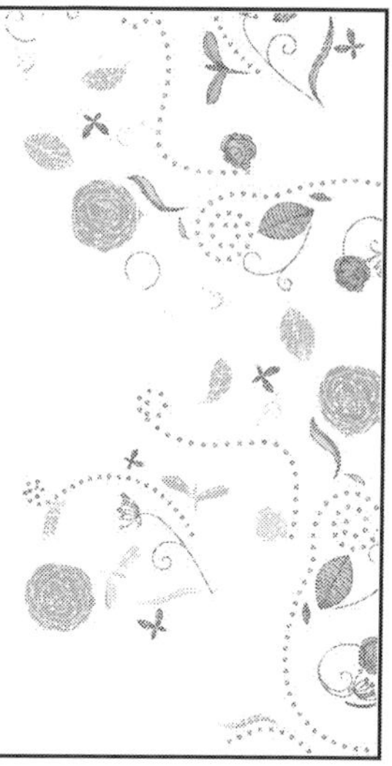

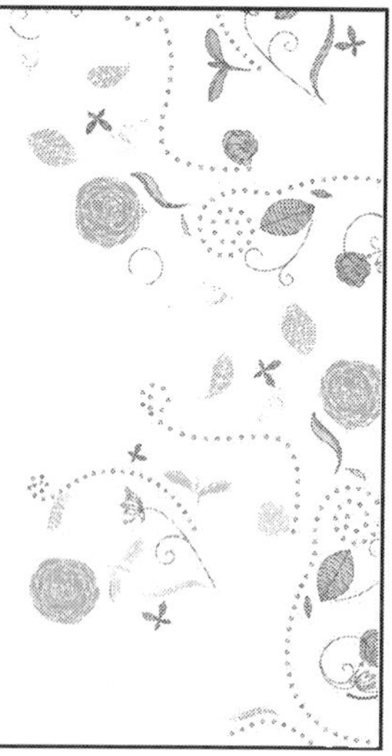

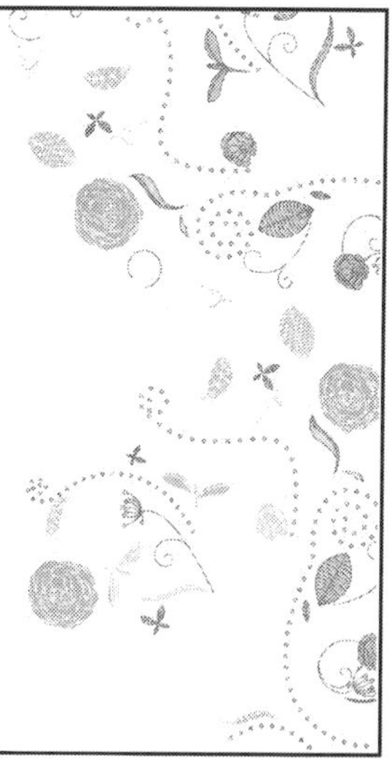

Printed in Great Britain
by Amazon

51458391R00063